HYDROPONICS FOR BEGINNERS:

Discover the Advantages of Hydroponics &
How to Develop an Unexpensive Solid System with
The Right Knowledge and Suitable Materials.
Build Your Healthy Garden Now!
(Part 1)

by **EMILY BATES**

Table Of Contents

PART 1

Introduction

The indoor gardening concept has been practiced since ancient times. Decorative plants make statements on the inside, but soon realized that people need to go into the sun, only the garden plows and see fresh flowers! Developed a series of indoor cultivation methods, as to give immediate access to gardener's herbs and fruits as well as the place of a plot leaves and flowers inside the house.

Indoor gardening, of course, began first with the ground as a medium. However, some studies have shown that the garden soil the most appropriate way may not be for interior gardening. According to the University of Illinois, garden soil diseases and parasites can contain that can cause damage to your houseplants. Mitigate the risk of diseases and pests should be modified, the soil of your garden, and should include a variety of media. Peat moss and for example, a beautiful indoor garden means they are free of diseases and pathogens and ensure proper ventilation and drainage.

The soil mix also depends on the type you want to grow the plants indoors. Herbs planted in containers gardens, for example, does not sit well with the peat soil mix, as they tend to lose moisture quickly. However, you can choose between different types of flower mixtures such as vermiculite, perlite, and pumice, or you can create your potting mix of organic material easily.

Another method of gardening is indoor hydroponics. Hydroponics is the "hydro" Greek and means "water" and "Ponos" meaning "work." The practice of hydroponics is already introduced in the 1950s, experimenting as some scientists with soluble nutrients in the water in the plant, rather than the nutrients from the soil. Although the growth and development of hydroponic were not so fast, now of their participation in the honor credit, the demand for food and fresh products increased and from the amount of fertile soil for planting.

Hydroponics has dipped its roots in a solution of water, where nutrients are mixed. The sources are in constant contact with these nutrients, rather than to find these nutrients in the soil. Since nutrients are available to cover the roots, the inner hydroponic gardening has provided a higher success rate available than most traditional gardening techniques.

Indoor gardening with soil and hydroponics can be quite tricky for beginner's gardener, but the rewards are worth it. The two media require maintenance in various aspects and levels of bred plants. For example, have different plants, different responses to varying degrees of light, and temperature—some plants, such as broccoli and cauliflower, as a fresh hydroponic garden.

The indoor gardening concept has been practiced since ancient times. Decorative plants make statements on the inside, but soon realized that people need to go into the sun, only the garden plows and see fresh flowers! Developed a series of indoor cultivation methods, as to give immediate access to gardener's herbs and fruits as well as the place of a plot leaves and flowers inside the house.

Indoor gardening, of course, began first with the ground as a medium. However, some studies have shown that the garden soil the most appropriate way may not be for interior gardening. According to the University of Illinois, garden soil diseases and parasites can contain that can cause damage to your houseplants. Mitigate the risk of diseases and pests should be modified, the soil of your garden, and should include a variety of media. Peat moss and for example, a beautiful indoor garden means they are free of diseases and pathogens and ensure proper ventilation and drainage.

The soil mix also depends on the type you want to grow the plants indoors. Herbs planted in containers gardens, for example, does not sit well with the peat soil mix, as they tend to lose moisture quickly. However, you can choose between different types of flower mixtures such as vermiculite, perlite, and pumice, or you can create your potting mix of organic material easily.

Another method of gardening is indoor hydroponics. Hydroponics is the "hydro" Greek and means "water" and "Ponos" meaning "work." The practice of hydroponics is already introduced in the 1950s, experimenting as some scientists with soluble nutrients in the water in the plant, rather than the nutrients from the soil. Although the growth and development of hydroponic were not so fast, now of their participation in the honor credit, the demand for food and fresh products increased and from the amount of fertile soil for planting.

Hydroponics has dipped its roots in a solution of water, where nutrients are mixed. The sources are in constant contact with these nutrients, rather than to find these nutrients in the soil. Since nutrients are available to cover the roots, the inner hydroponic gardening has provided a higher success rate available than most traditional gardening techniques.

Indoor gardening with soil and hydroponics can be quite tricky for beginner's gardener, but the rewards are worth it. The two media require maintenance in various aspects and levels of bred plants. For example, have different plants, different responses to varying degrees of light, and temperature. Some plants, such as broccoli and cauliflower, as a fresh hydroponic garden. While some varieties do not produce heads that enough for your taste, broccoli and cauliflower are great to tend hydroponic flavorful and tender their soil varieties.

Some plants, such as various lighting systems. A garden with potting soil mixed stuffed tomatoes can grow well in full sun as well as its varieties are hydroponically grown hydroponic plants, however, tend to have more water and nutrients from your deposit lick as they grow.

If you are considering starting an indoor garden, whether, with soil and hydroponics as a means, it is best to first the type of plants and their needs to understand, this can help extend the growing season and provide plenty of fresh produce throughout the year.

Science has always pushed forward in improving the lives of people. Every day, scientists spend hours trying to improve current living conditions or to create new ones that are better than what is currently getting. Find out to make fun of ways for our efficient processes.

This simple guide for implementation ultimately crashes hydroponic your best choice if you want. Being an essential part of the future of agriculture, understand the intricacies of hydroponics requires expert advice. This book will. By the type of practice, the best forms of hydroponics and more

Hydroponic gardening is an excellent way for your garden fruits and vegetables to maintain throughout the year. It also means that they will grow not exposed to pesticides, chemicals, and the rigors of shipping long distances; these factors can slow and vegetable nutrient content and flavor of the fruit.

The productivity of hydroponic gardening can work, if properly prepared and informed to overcome by their relatively simple application, in terms of understanding the ease with which it, you can start your garden.

Soil hydroponic gardening is necessary. The water is all the required light, nutrients. For a beginner, it is essential to know precisely what you need in terms of the expected results and what kind of space you have. Provide visiting local storage, forums, and search blogs and as many questions as possible.

Hydroponic gardening has many advantages over traditional methods of cultivation makes hydroponic garden soil-base that will never thank you for the environment, no matter where you are STAY-hydroponic gardening no seasons.

Where do you could get freezing, and indeed, hydroponic garden thrives if you have the right light, temperature, nutrients, and moisture?

If you can help these factors, either in a small cabinet the size of the system or a massive target conservatory, you can enjoy tropical fruits and vegetables out of season all year round! Hydroponic fruits and vegetables are usually larger than their natural counterparts, more edible food.

Hydroponics is still a uniform quantity of food and maximized with nutrients and oxygen it provides. Never the facility lack of essential nutrients and this is growing much faster at a controlled temperature, with the garden and its contents that a classic essential garden soil to ideal weather conditions and many other factors without greenhouse based.

They should be treated with a variety of pesticides and other chemicals never that hydroponically grown fruits and vegetables fruits and vegetables are often used in growth in trade; this only nutritional value much higher guarantee.

This technique of "pure" combined with the fact that the performance of you should not go over your kitchen porch hydroponic system - consumes Vegetables has not gone hundreds of miles and save your shipping loss and the severity of the traffic.

All these excellent benefits come at a price. To establish the cost of a hydroponic garden are expensive first in many ways, but once you have configured, the system can be administered at a reasonable price. If your goal is simple and to live alone on their hydroponic production, it is likely to spend much money to start.

Of course, the available space would also be a factor in how you can develop at any time. Once the hydroponic system is configured correctly, the plants grow bigger and faster; they easily exceed the space where the assigned initially, so you should space if you overestimate the first time.

Hydroponic gardening is safe, inexpensive, and relatively easy! However, it is the same that any initiative, the time, and resources it deserves is simply a matter of proper planning and forecasting all the facts in advance and know the variables before buying any hardware to be seen.

If you want to grow plants or greenhouse worthy entire meal, hydroponic make you eat well all year round, you never grocery go shopping again!

This is to learn the perfect guide to the basics of hydroponics as a beginner in the garden. I hope you make the best use.

Let us start!

CHAPTER 1:

What Is Hydroponics

Word hydroponics comes from the Greek for "the work of the water," which is a strategy for the development of plants in liquid rich in place in soil nutrients.

Probably the best of hydroponics is fine, maybe in a room a modest false or veranda, a small yard, the roof of a tall building, and inside. As an independent system, a hydroponic table can to all the estimates are revised, that you (the water remembers weight) to accommodate you and a companion or family.

Hydroponics can be defined without soil for the cultivation of plants as a technique (not ground). This strategy uses more soluble minerals in the water that nutrients dunning possible to be more productive when the field is used.

This should be possible in good weather or inside the year and has many favorable circumstances, including:

· No weeding

· Rapid development

· High yields in a small space

· No bugs under crops

· Washing vegetables

· Ease of harvest

· Consistent quality

· No errors or floor disorders

There are several types or varieties of hydroponics.

Hydroponics is it for human food producers and business specialist's suitable gardener. Hydroponics, some favorable circumstances has a dirty way. Unlike corn in the ground, in a hydroponic system, grown plants do not create large structures analysis root for nutrients. It is the examination, and pH levels forced easier. In the art of hydroponics, plants are raised in an inert medium and adjusted to develop pH smoothly, must consume the plants' only negligible vitality from the roots to get nutrients. Energy stored by the sources is better spent on the production of fruit and flowers.

In hydroponic vegetable crops, they have improved in a fair environment (such as balls or mudstone). At this time, a layout cluster is removed, all the essential nutrients the plant has needs. This fluid flows around the food and then the underlying principles of the plants either (inactive) by extrusion type or a siphon (dynamic). Presto! A final development machines!

Dynamic systems in which the juice is diverted into the plant is very productive. It is ideal for the development of a fully automated piece or child care. In hydroponics, all you do is give nutrients legitimate fundamentals of a plant is based. The roots cannot take unmixed components. They do not absorb the floor. The plant does not care where it gets its essential product synthesis, either soil or hydroponic agreement.

In a hydroponic garden, your floor with everything you need care in several extensions, at the right time in the most efficient manner. Is this an attempt to develop the "perfect soil" to achieve their full genetic potential? Also, with the best equipment, supplies, and some stability can be a good come close, darn.

Some people accept that hydroponic plants developed "steroids" or other dangerous hormones so good to do and looked as if surprising. Add no, not destructive nutrients arrangements hydroponic synthetic compounds. We provide our plants with the same 17 nutrients and components appearance of the plant in the ground. Also, each plant uses only specific components that you need, either from the ground or arrangement.

A brief history of hydroponic garden

instead of terrestrial plants growing in water, hanging an ancient practice dating back gardens of Babylon. The Chinese used this method in ancient times; They were in ancient times famous for its "floating gardens." Although the prevailing theory behind hydroponic is always the same, modern technology has given us faster, grow faster, and safe plants.

It has been in modern times, the process of soilless by Francis Bacon in a book called "Sylva Sylvarum," published in 1627 described, was one of the first-mentioned that in European literature methods on the ground agriculture. Between 1627 and 1860, the cultivation of plants in water was more sophisticated and something to be demystified.

While scientists to experiment with different kinds have begun to grow plants in water, they have the techniques to become more refined. It has been found that the water with nutrients size greater reach than usual, could be mixed to help plants. These first attempts to understand the methods were considered "culture solution. "Is used this term commonly used as a general term for hydroponic gardening by the scientific community until 1920. Today, the term" culture solution is "used to describe the growing of plants in a non-growth material for liquid stabilizes the roots.

Hydroponic gardening, as we know it today, is based on these initial efforts and continues to evolve and change as more research and tests conducted. Today, technological advances have almost every allowed reaping the rewards over the ground growth.

The term "hydroponics" was from an employee of Dr. invented Gericke doctor WA Satchell professor of botany at the University of California, who suggested that "Hydroponics is the griego'hidro" or water, there's ponos', or the work is already comparable designated geoponics had in agriculture before.

Thus, on February 12, 1937, the term "hydroponics" was presented in an article in the journal Science, "... in the sense of growing vegetables, fruit, and flowers without soil the public, the reservoirs fertilized hot water.

Of course, they asked the public, as well as many contemporaries William, this allegation.

His critics were wrong as Gericke's experience with tomatoes produced 25 feet tall vine tomatoes with water and nutrients.

Because of the surprising results show Gericke, a much more detailed analysis was carried out by scientists at the University of California and continue to demonstrate the benefits of growing plants without soil.

One of the first commercial applications was conducted for Hydroponics 1934. This year, Pan Am Rookie chose Wake Iceland as one of several stations for island road to the Far East hopping for its fleet of seaplanes expansion. The new service was added in 1935, and the following year the construction of housing for the crew and passengers had required while the aircraft was seen on decks 10 to 12 hours. These hotels also hungry travelers had to meet, and the islands are little more than rocky atolls, all conducive to the cultivation of traditional crops. Powerboats twice a year,

In 1937, T. LAMORY Laumeister, a senior at the University of the Ministry of Agriculture, a partner Gericke California, travel selected Wake Island an experience in vegetable crops to create, with hydroponics. The original goal was too fresh vegetables for 35 permanent islanders and reacted to produce to the growing number of passengers.

From 1937 to 1941 LAMORY and Torrey Lyon designed the hydroponic structures and beds more 230 square meters of wooden baths on 1,000 square meters, including the growth of concrete foundations red and dissolved, and the problems of production and had enough grain to feed the growing population and the hotel guests

On December 8, 1941, after the Japanese attacked Pearl Harbor, Wake Iceland was also attacked and occupied. Fortunately, all employees and the employees of the outbreak of war were evacuated, and the Japanese use of hydroponic beds during the occupation of the islands.

In addition to large nutritious fruits and vegetables, this offers a modern hydroponic garden gardener?

How it works hydroponics

We have already found that, contrary to traditional farming where the ground support installation, so that remain to

And a supply of nutrients, in hydroponic plants have provided an artificial medium and solution containing all the necessary nutrients. The idea behind the hydroponic installation is simple. It is believed that environmental factors often limit plant growth, and thus a solution deliver nutrients to plant roots contains the gardener optimum constant supply of nutrients and water supplies. Nutritional efficiency is a plant to its full potential so that it is more productive.

The solution, which is rich in nutrients in several ways:

- In the first, the plants are placed in an inert substance and sometimes flooded roots with the solution.

- Secondly, Plants can be placed on the inert materials and the answer on the bottom with a drip solution rain.

- The third option Place the plants in a slightly superior film to solve so that plant roots

- The fourth means are floating, and the plant roots in the air and the roots are sometimes sprayed with a mist of the solution.

All the methods described above are using the machine to do one or the other, or by a nebulizer, with the use of, or use of a pump for supplying the solution from the storage area. The solution had been well ventilated so that the roots of the oxygen they need, as soon as the solution obtained turns. Plants require energy to absorb the mineral solution, and the absorption process requires energy, which is made possible by breathing.

Is it tough?

Indeed, the creation and maintenance of a hydroponic system can be a difficult task. The plants need a variety of nutrients, and the optimal amount of each nutrient varies. Also, the nutritional needs will change from each plant as it moves through various stages of development. To use local conditions such as water hardness too much importance.

It is also a fact that some nutrients are absorbed into the ground much faster than others, which may cause the accumulation of specific ions in the solution, therefore, a change in the pH of the solution. After the assignment pH, the uptake of other nutrients by the plant is hindered due to the absorption of certain nutrients at the pH-dependent, and because excess availability of specific nutrients prevents the absorption of others. For example, if ammonia.

This content is very high; the calcium absorption and, also, excess calcium decreases the intake is reduced by magnesium.

Another important aspect is to ensure that the elements react to form compounds that are difficult to absorb, which means they must be made at different times available.

With several variations on a hydroponic farmer has put together a good understanding of the needs of the plants and the interaction of nutrients, and with the same plants. You must carefully monitor and review to the concentration changes occur, the proposed solutions for the plants. The alternative is that the farmer in automated hydroponics to invest, which is quite expensive to manage the process on their behalf.

Farmers are also conscientious about preventing the solutions with undesirable substances contamination are used necessary. Most choose the hydroponic project in a greenhouse or to connect a building to ensure that they only what happens in the control systems. This limitation makes it possible to optimize the freedom of farmers to environmental influences in plants, such as carbon dioxide exposure and light temperatures, while income maximizes received.

This means that hydroponics is used not only on the growth of plants without soil; This also means that the farmer has full control of the plant and its growth process, at least.

You can grow

If this type can grow by miracle cultures through the hydroponic system, the simple answer is that you can grow vegetables, fruits, or indoor plants. The system, however, is most suitable for crops that can grow well in hydroponic conditions.

The general rule is that the use of a solution is better for the plants; the roots tend to have something more.

For example, you can lettuce, radishes, herbs, or spinach grown. Aggregate systems are best suited for crops, a deep root system that sugar beet has, and those whose peaks are to be substantial in general, such as cucumbers and squash.

Could plant other plants tomatoes, strawberries, peppers, celery, and watercress are.

tomato Varieties are especially popular in this type of farming, bear fruit, says growing and

Indeterminate, meaning they grow continuously and repeatedly. Always refer to fruits on their stems.

Farmers are generally resistant to disease, even to lean varieties of crop plants because plants live longer and produce therefore longer.

Avoid that are not genetically adapted to environmental hydroponic wheat plants.

The researchers found that the development of enough wheat for bread should be less than $ 23! It is too expensive.

The advantages of hydroponics

Plants were grown hydroponically reason are often higher than their adult counterparts have ground to do with the fact that the absorption of nutrients through a liquid solution is much more efficient process of the plant that the earth; the food is more comfortable to digest, in a sense. Because of this ease of absorption, hydroponic plants more than fifty per cent have grown more than plants in the ground usually! Some of the other advantages of hydroponics are:

• Crop yields are also bright, and the nutrient content is often higher than the same plant grows in a more traditional way increase. It is not just to get more fruits and vegetables with hydroponic gardening, healthier forever!

• To create a garden that is possible, even in areas where there is no ground. This means that you can grow live as condominiums and apartment plants in space. It also opens the possibility to convert the building on several plots' full levels of agriculture.

• You can grow food in places that are traditionally not suitable for agriculture and drylands. Israel and Arizona have adopted this technique of cultivation so that the citizens of adults eating at home enjoy and to expand its food market. It also allows remote and inaccessible that no agricultural land, such as Bermuda, their own cultures grow. Areas such as

Alaska and Russia, the short seasons for planting have, have also adopted in hydroponic greenhouses, and added they that better control of the time might have for your plants.

- Maintain your hydroponic installation is more comfortable than to take care of garden soil. They tend to use less water, appear intuitive-cons like

Because the plants are grown in water. However, this implementation is always reused water.

- A proper pH to obtain is also more natural. Moreover, it is to ensure that crops receive adequate nutrition they need and deserve.

- Parasites are often less afraid and those who find their way, they are easier to treat.

- Harvesting of vegetables is often more comfortable if the hydroponic process.

In examining the benefits mentioned above, you might think, "What's the catch? "He must be a downside here, right? More popular and customary otherwise would hydroponics. Hydroponics may seem complicated, the thick veil of jargon scares many people away before they begin a chance to experience how easy it can be, hydroponic plants to grow.

CHAPTER 2:

Hydroponic Garden Cons

With the advantages, you will always disadvantage. Let us look at them!

The high cost of setting up

Hydroponics has circumcised a higher start-up cost, the cultivated soil. You have a few items to get started:

A water reservoir

A water pump recirculation

A set-up for their plant growth (NFT, DWC) culture medium nutrient

(Sometimes the artificial light sources)

Diseases of the air

Although the risk of foodborne illnesses is low on the ground, the disease can occur in the air, and because of the nature of hydroponics, these diseases can spread quickly in plants as they are planted near them.

It is essential to be aware of the main signs of plant diseases to be and respond as quickly as possible.

Another example of a disease that is not in the air, Pythium (root rot), which can be used in a hydroponic system, to the water, and the result used the browning of the roots. Fortunately, you can control most of them by appropriate design of the system.

CHAPTER 3:

Knowledge

To understand the principles behind hydroponics is relatively simple, although some learning is required. However, the system is running correctly; you must involve the various devices and how to control understand and adjust nutrient content.

To get this right is essential to create a long-term system, but a steep learning curve can be. If you are the first time, they failed to see it as a learning experience and not as a defeat.

CHAPTER 4:

At sight

When plant growth is based using conventional methods in the field, you can leave your plants for several days. Nature has a habit, a way to grow for help in finding plants in almost any situation.

If you created a hydroponic system, you should consider whether there are visible problems and often check nutritional content.

To have a mechanical failure, a very negative impact can have on your hydroponic system that could kill your plants!

Of course, there are more ways to automate parts of the system, but this should not be your primary concern when the first system is created hobby.

CHAPTER 5:

Electricity

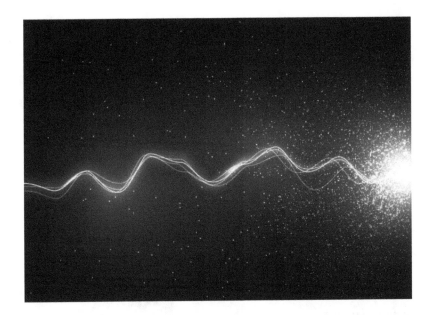

A stream is essential to operate pumps, adjusting the supply of artificial light, heating or cooling, and the air movement. All these additions lead to higher electricity bills, which is an additional cost.

Water and electricity are generally not good, making it a safety risk you must consider.

If something happens to the electricity grid, plants can suffer surprisingly fast. You need a backup option you have the pump for a few hours in a trading system to run. This can be done with a solar system or a backup generator.

There are several types of hydroponic development strategies, including:

- Nutrient Film Strategy (NFT)

- Bits system

- Fluctuations (floods and channel)

- The culture of water

- Drip System

- Aeroponic system

Aquaponics is the United hydroponics with aquaculture (fish farming).

This should be possible in good weather or inside the year and has many favourable circumstances, including:

- No weeding

- The rapid development

- High performance in a small space

- Not taking beings cultures

• Wash vegetables

• Simple collection

• Consistent quality

• No illnesses to the ground or crawling creatures related

Perhaps the best thing about hydroponics is that it tends in a gallery or a small courtyard, a small yard, the roof of a tall building, and to do inside. As an independent system, a hydroponic table to the size that you (do not forget the water weight) will be adjusted to accommodate you and a companion or family.

Given the amount of money you must spend, the plants need to grow, and how you should go to the board, there are many alternatives to look over. Avoid making mistakes outrageous to do some exploring and select the technology that is right for you and your place.

CHAPTER 6:

Dynamic Through Independent Hydroponic Systems

There are a variety of types of hydroponic systems. However, most are considered active or latent are. The system uses traps in the water, while an order does not involve gravity fluid moves or uses a wicking material to use to draw water to the roots.

Whether dynamic or far, most hydroponics at home are closed systems that recycle nutrients several times to conserve available water through the system. In an open order, water is not detected and reused.

CHAPTER 7:

Based systems Media

lthough plants can grow in water for large plants like tomatoes, it is useful to have help for established plants as a means of development.

There are many types of media in latent development that can be used for pre-established conservation. Inclusion sand base substrates, rock, polyethylene fiber, pea stone, coconut fiber, perlite, vermiculite, the base granules, glass beads, and stone wool.

To keep them moist media development, one of the support systems are commonly used:

• A locking system is one of the strategies based on the most basic means of communication, acts as self-irrigation support. Pieces of cotton or nylon rope direct air through the provision of deposition nutrient use of thin free-flowing into the plant growth medium above are found, the latent moisture providing plants. This system works best for plants that do not require as herbs such as rosemary, thyme, and oregano, as soon as microgreens development and deeply established plants, such as beets and radishes, plenty of water.

• A rollback movement or flooding system and the channels can be dynamic or inactive, depending on how much work to do. The roots with water in time offer, usually regularly twice a day, then let channeling away. This can physically by water is carried from one side of the system in a container later removed from the media and pour again on the very edge of the system a few hours after the fact. This type of system box fetched without far and pipes connected computerize using a dip siphon to a clock, which is the water to move, to convert it to an operating system.

• The drip systems are also dynamic. They provide a constant flow of water to each plant through an infusion line. Water overabundance optional below the storage container downwards and again filtered through a siphon back through the infusion line is returned.

CHAPTER 8:

Fluid systems based

Fluid-based systems are used no media development assistance to the roots of plants. Instead, the plants are suspended in pots or other network structures, that the underlying principles hold presented in an array of nutrients supplied air by a vacuum device type aquarium.

• The techniques of nutrient films (NFT) poor air film train continuously flows through the plant nutrients by a triggering even tilted system. The plants are exposed in the openings with the highest point of the channels, and nutrients are returned to the upper part of each trough and flow by gravity to the lower end of the turn, are deflected by the circle.

• In deep water hydroponics, plants and their underlying fundamentals depend on several nutrients. Kind of technology jetty, slide polystyrene foam boards on the outside of the water. Openings cut into the reinforcing mesh Styrofoam pots and protect sink in water. The plants develop their submerged foundations in air through the available nutrients in the dock flows. This is a fantastic development strategy lettuce, herbs, and other light yields not quite overwhelming grow the boats to sink.

Quality and fertilizer water

Since water is the most critical component in hydroponics, she tries before you start. Synthetic Found in tap water may not be safe for your plants, and minerals convergence can affect the balance of the compost.

Although you can mix your own, there is two natural and synthetic fertilizer specifically for the development of hydroponic systems. Some are used exclusively for the development of green corn, while others described the development of flowers and fruits. The use of the proposed garden compost for use in soil not produce the ideal growth of plants and can clog pipes and equipment.

An arrangement somewhat acidic (5.5 to 6.5) is ideal for plant-available nutrients to try to use the pH of the constant disposal.

So, the nutrients believed I come, add water to keep the degree of relentless desire for change and keep the constant desire again. Remember that some plants have different needs, and you will have to change their arrangement nutrients in the same way.

CHAPTER 9:

The Plants In Hydroponic Systems

To ensure the possibility that you buy for the plants to the root wash dirt that you can purchase the soil diseases. One of the pleasures of gardening is to organize hydroponic ground; you do not have any problems with stress on illness. Primary health practices hold, help without disadvantages of the system.

Rapid growth rates for some crops such as lettuce, chard, arugula, and green prison various pests, built them.

Randomly develop your plants from seed, you can start filled with a soilless mix of peat pellets, 3d squares of rock wool or connectors that drive. Move the hydroponic system, if the roots have become through the base of the attachment.

Fertilization is a problem if they develop within fruit plants. In the garden air, tomatoes are pollinated by the wind. Mimic the inside, a fan or tap running, and the vines shake when the bud. Search autógamas cucumber tied with each female flower.

Or buy DIY?

It is slightly less challenging to flow your hydroponic system essential to building plastic tray storage to use a pneumatic machine for the air through the intake of nutrients or help to plunge siphon circle and development of liquid media or net pots plants, For those achieved by working with PVC pipes, space-saving design, the many plants and carry water can be developed to keep from one end to the other. (Ramos cards can be found on the Internet.)

CHAPTER 10:

Types Of Garden Hydroponic

HYDROPONICS SYSTEM TYPES

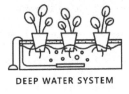

DEEP WATER SYSTEM

WICK SYSTEM

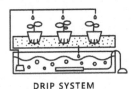

DRIP SYSTEM

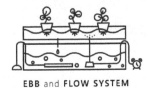

EBB and FLOW SYSTEM

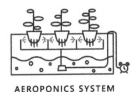

AEROPONICS SYSTEM

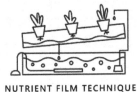

NUTRIENT FILM TECHNIQUE

How can appear confused hydroponic systems work from the beginning, but as soon as they arrive, they will perceive how the work is straightforward. There are six main types of hydroponic systems (drip, ebb, and flow, NFT Hydroponic, aeroponics, and wick). Plant roots need three things, water/moisture, nutrients, and oxygen. What makes the six distinctive types of hydroponic systems is simply the way they transmitted these three roots of the plant. Each type of system is described in detail in part (by name) on the side and bottom.

Despite what they may decide to call them, each hydroponic system depends on these six types, and these two types of systems, or a mixture of at least two of the six classes. There are several approaches varieties and change parts of the six types of systems. So, if you know how each of the three roots needs (water, nutrients, and oxygen) are transported to any kind of hydroponic system, you can quickly have the option of this type can be seen from the system, any hydroponic it is.

CHAPTER 11:

The six types of hydroponic systems

1. drip system

2. Ebb-flow (flood and drain)

3. NFT (nutrient film technique)

4. Hydroponic

5. aeroponic

6. Wick system

Do they say nothing about aquaponics?

Some will say that aquaponics another type of hydroponic system. Anyway, aquaponics is usually not the seventh type of hydroponic system that essentially makes distinctive aquaponics Disputes how the nutrients are calculated. As nutrients transported to the roots. Aquaponic process and deliver nutrients from decaying fish waste can replace the standard deposition nutrients to be used in one of the six types of hydroponic systems fish tank for storing.

There is much more to aquaponics than light, because their attempt to reduce the content of microorganisms usually specific nutrients, microscopic organisms, and life to control the little vegetation in the reservoir water, can use waste to break fish nutrients that plants. Aquaponics is a waste of manufacturing nutrients, primarily fish, to create their nutrients. Anyway, it has transported to the plant roots will not affect the way water, nutrients, oxygen, and.

Before you design and build a hydroponic system

Before a hydroponic system to make, it is essential first to consider the type of plants you need to develop and the space it needs for its development. Currently, you need a point to structure the system is the ability to meet the needs of the plant (to force plant height, root pruning, oxygen to the roots, the use of water, and so on and so on.) Well, above the average size to reach. Although a type of hydroponic system is suitable for the development of certain types of plants, it may not be the best decision for another event.

Some things you need to remember when structuring and construction (in all cases, purchase), each hydroponic system; First, you will probably use more than once, you should look at things like the way it will be difficult for cleaning all together to separate between plantings and remove. Similarly, if you have a problem, while the plants are still in development, it is essential to consider them, it will be challenging to solve the issues without damaging the plant or system.

You can convert almost all kinds of plants in hydroponic system design if the system needs the plant not to force structured, in any case, when they reach full size. Despite everything, it may be more comfortable, less support, and to develop less expensive than in another hydroponic system. Also, in the development of many types of plants, it is best to improve continuously for these returns in different orders, rather than trying to create thanks to the extensive card system.

CHAPTER 12:

The Hydroponic System Requires Only A Few Basics In Buildings

The developing chamber (or plate)

The developing room is part of the hydroponic system where the roots of the plant grow. The developing chamber support for the root zone. This region supports plants, such as roots, the available nutrients. Similarly, it protects the roots from light, heat, and noise. It is essential to keep the area of the current source and light tests.

Designed to the sources in light damage and high temperatures in the root zone heating plants is related cause by stress waiver heat on fruits and flowers.

The size and condition of the device revealed that it depends significantly on the type of hydroponic system structure, such as the type of plants that grow in it. The upper floors have more extensive root systems and require more space to keep them. The structures are unlimited in time here. Almost anything can be used as a developing chamber, simply preferred not to use anything metal, or could consume nutrients or meet them. If you check out, we get thoughts of what undoubtedly groups, and as can a variety of things use to the development councils to build your hydroponic system.

I repository

The deposit is part of the hydroponic system that keeps the nutrients. The device comprises a plant nutrient, which is mixed in water. This depends on the type of hydroponic system, the supply of nutrients can power the camera (rhizosphere) development cycles siphon using a clock, and the clock is running continuously, or the roots can even hanging down at the store all day, to make every day, including the submission of developing chamber.

You can make something a plastic tent containing water. For a long time, enough water to share and everything cleaned, it tends to be used as a reservoir. You were leafing through this book more about how much your nutrients should be a repository. Its memory confirmation must light. If you can stand on your head and understand something clearly, at last, coming through it, it is not to check the view. Anyway, it is less hard not to do something the easy confirmation holds paint, covering, wrapping or something like protection time of the airbag on them.

Submersible pump,

Most systems use a diving hydroponic siphon to water (nutrient availability) of the bearing in the bedroom/pull for plant development. The submersible siphon can, in a hydroponic supply store, is much of a stretch with no or at most hardware stores in the house with objects as the source of gardening and the lake also siphon. Similarly, they come in a variety of sizes. Browse previous size siphon to choose your need for your hydroponic system?

SUBMERSIBLE siphons are just a drive that used to convert an electromagnet substantially. You can also effectively all cleaned wholly disassembled. Otherwise accompanies a channel, you can without much of a stretch to cut an adjustment chain of comparisons heating or screen materials. You must keep cleaning both the trap and the channel regularly to keep it clean.

Transport system

A system of water management Transport/nutrients is very simple and incredibly adaptable to mount its water systems. Additionally, Siphon is simply plucked the experience/nutrient solution to find water one possible set of rhythm in the developing chamber and the tank. In general, more natural, and better materials for the nutrient transport system can be used PVC blend and line style connector, wherein the network of standard garden water pipes and connectors, such as vinyl tubes dark blue you.

Does it depend on the type of hydroponic system installed, you can drop by drop or spray manufacturers as an essential aspect of your nutrient transport management system must use? While they can be useful, which also clog. So that you do the chance, make sure that you have additional items you can trade clogged clean so quickly. Manufacturers are trying not as a stop to use, up to the actual additional costs correspond.

Simple timer,

It depends on the type of hydroponic system you manufacture and where the system is set to expand its facilities. You may need a few simple watches. If you develop fake plants, use light instead of light characteristic of the day, a watch is required to switch the opportunities on controlling / off for the lighting system. Filling and channel, aeroponic, and drip systems, you need a clock / control the hiking off siphon immersion water. Some types of aeroponic systems may require only a watch. Visits aeroponic methods for business and leisure on the types of aeroponic systems and watch for them.

Standard periodic light watches work well for the two lamps in the same way as siphons retractable. However, we prescribe to make sure that the clock is designed for 15 amps instead of 10 amperes. Fifteen amplifier watches regularly called essential; If not, check the back of the package or the timer to 15 amps. Similarly, try to get outside use, usually has a gap, and are generally drinking water.

We do not write the most expensive watches online progressed a kind. Primarily, because the computer clock, all the memories are free, the same as the settings on the possibility that free or separated, in each case for one second under all conditions (except for energy if you see an extra Battery). They often have no more true start/stop type that merely. Make sure the clock has sticks to move the region.

An air motor,

Also, to grow in water systems, pneumatic machines are discretionary in hydroponic systems. However, the use of them has advantages and power equipment are modest terms. The vacuum unit is everywhere aquarium supplies sales. Machines just pneumatic air supply and oxygen to form water and roots. The air is deflected by an aircraft air stone that much small air do that climb through the amount of nutrients bubbles.

Cultivation systems in water, the air pump keeps the roots of the plant in suffocation in nutrient availability immersed every minute of every day. For another hydroponic system, the vacuum apparatus is used provided regularly. It helps in the expansion of the oxygen content in the water; it breaks down and keeps the hydrogen peroxide. Visit this site collapsed gradually on the oxygen content.

Other pieces of pneumatic Leeway's machines are used to keep the air in the water and nutrients bubbles in motion and turn what the nutrients keep mixing continuously. The disease also takes hydrogen peroxide coursed positive balance to increase in the repository.

Developing lights

Developing lights are discretion hydroponic systems. It depends on where you put your hydroponics and grow crops. You can decide

DIFFERENT HYDROPONICS

1. THE drip system

Hydroponic drip systems

Drip systems are one of the most widely used worldwide in hydroponic systems, both for the manufacturer as for commercial producers in the same house right kinds. This is mainly because it is a simple idea and needs almost everywhere, but is a versatile and convincing way hydroponic system. Even though this is a simple idea, it does not limit your creativity when their policies produced. Like a drip system is a bit like the sound works, only drip nutrients available to plant roots it moist to keep.

Hydroponic drip systems can, without much of a stretch, be prepared in many ways, just as the large orders. Either way, your valuable, especially for large plants that have plenty of room for the roots. This is because you do not interfere with large amounts of water; the system and drip lines are anything but difficult, which run on more areas to flood. On the same as if a means of possibilities of developing a more develop for larger systems, as small amounts retain more moisture used and is particularly suitable for large installations because it is much more forgiving plants.

What you need is a drip system to do:

• A primary underlying compartment of the plant to grow.

• A chamber (power) to keep the supply of nutrients.

• A submersible fountain/siphon lake.

• A clock-killing light and stop.

• Some pipes run siphon power plants (as well as drip lines in the possibility of remote sizes use).

• pipe (PVC or a flexible tube), running to the finish line for the additional supply of nutrients in the repository.

• (optional) can be used by manufacturers, drop by drop, or just openings, small puncture on the tube nutrient reaction cutting paper drip hot as we do like.

• Substrates for plant roots to develop and help to strengthen the weight of the plant.

A drop of a hydroponic drip system is secure. Water (nutrients available) deviates upwardly from the store through the tube at the highest point of the media in the development (where the plant roots are); from that point, it flows on the machine on the growth medium. The disposition of depleted nutrients injected the roots both down and to assist the media in the correct Base Development. From this moment, the supply of nutrients flows through an aperture / s, and the answer of gravity allows nutrients in the repository on the right side through the tube to trickle down. It is important to remember that the plants should be in the development field in all cases,

There are two types of extreme gout systems hydroponic drip.

Recycling drop by drop systems / Recreation

be used for the domestic manufacturers, recycling systems Drip by far, the most common. Drip recycling systems are like what it sounds like. Simply refers to nutrient recovery/disposal of used bicycles to wet roots in the repository where it can be easily recycled into the system and used repeatedly. Recycling systems recovery systems, they are also the nutrients available in accordance invited used to retrieve that tends to be back recycled through the system.

Changed to the same as any other hydroponic system, which drips nutrient availability of recycling, both can be recovered in the pH values of equal quality nutrients that the plant nutrients flowing spend in the water repeatedly. Along these lines, recycling systems make it necessary occasionally to check and change the variable pH, as the nutrients regularly just to keep the same AC available nutrient reaction plants.

No collection recycling drip systems /

For partners, the drip systems without recycling/recovery, they are not usually healthy. Although it seems a water belly and nutrients do not recover and reuse, commercial producers practically nothing stomach. They do it coordinated with their precision irrigation cycles. With only "cadenzas" that the dilution can vary widely, so times or even seconds have to luck to do it. You long enough to water to the media in development. Thus, water (nutrients available) drip consumed on plants and produced in the center were to achieve the growth of plant roots, and virtually no case slips. From time to time,

drop the supply of nutrients in drip systems without recycling/recovery is not, in general, less support, mainly because of the action, none of the available nutrients used reused in the store again. This means you can use the tank with a fair, nutrients pH balance available and will not fill change, so you do not have that keep watch. For a more extended period, offers the water remains gradually moving / dogs so that the heavy mineral components sit on the floor. Still, a decent pH balanced nutrient availability.

2. Ebb and flow (flood and drain) SYSTEM

Ebb and Flow - System (also known as flooding and drainage).

The flood and drain systems (ebb and flow) are known for producing hydroponic any reason house. In addition to simple, they are for anyone to manufacture, it can be virtually any material used it to build with, so you do not go over a lot of money to develop hydroponic plants. Likewise, you can fit in any room to work (either inside or outside) may have, and there are no restrictions on innovative approaches and extraordinary plans for this space. With the construct to be economical and comfortable, the plants are excellent systems and sewer flooding. The system floods and channel function primarily as seeming like it, mostly with the nutrients the root system flooding of plants. Intermittently rather than continuously.

How do a hydroponic system and spillway channel work very merely? The cornerstone of the order of flooding and the channel compartments plants. It is perfect, maybe just a plant or multiple plants/owner of the provision. Again, clock role in the siphon and water (nutrients available) is through the tube from the reservoir within the central part of the system is deflected a diving source siphon/lake using. The supply of nutrients or fill (flooding), the system until it reaches the height of the overflow pipe preset to soak the roots of the plant.

When the water/flood filling the system reaches the height of the overflow tube, drains to foods, where it is again returned through the arrangement.

The overflow pipe placed the height of the water level in the flood system, and the channel, such as water (nutrient availability) provides, not at the highest point of the system to flow, while the siphon is on. Currently, bottom guides provide water flow through the siphon (System damaging).

What you need to build a flood and drain systems (ebb and flow):

- A primary underlying compartment of the plant to grow.

- A chamber (store) to the feed to keep nutrients.

- A submersible fountain/siphon lake.

- A clock-killing light and stop.

- Some courses run lines from the mains to prevent flooding.

- Several overflow pipes in the air you need the water level.

- The increase mechanism or something like that.

There is a wide range of approaches to a system build from flooding and the channel and is developing ordinarily excellent small medium-sized plants. In any case, for the development of large systems with large structures and channel flooding. Use almost anything to make crates pipes, 2-liter bottles, collection bags, water bottles, an old refrigerator, garbage, etc. almost anything that can hold water can be used one. The creative spirit is not all. There are many approaches roots flood and drain and the system.

Sure, it is a way to air the highest point of wealth water without spilling enter (Tip 1) Make it. A connector "T" with an extension that is pleasant a pair of tracks on the work of the waterline. This will form air pockets in the system and cause flooding and, therefore, suitable, avoid strenuously.

(Tip 2) Ensure that the overflow pipe to the cylinder chamber of the water trap. In any case, if the water only by gravity, and the water comes from the weight of the evidence that more water could redirect the overflow coming out at the end. This will spill the development of the fast water and the highest point on the system if you reduce the weight (volume) of the siphon.

There are three types of agreements and flood channels.

Compartments in the plant layout structure

This type of arrangement is used regularly when (flooded) with a wide range of substrates with plants simultaneously sprayed. It is imperative that the plant system to remember (compartments), which was flooded (irrigated), be on a table or a seat on the deposit needs. Thus, the water can flow by gravity to the reservoir, and thus effectively the system channel.

First, many media are fully involved all through the tube so that when the system is flooded to flood, and at once. For fatigue-rather than for each carrier overflow with various is flooded, there is a pipe overflow in the rule. It is connected to the base system, are connected in which all carrier. Besides, when the sculpture water reached its highest point of overflow, it overflows and returns to the store through the system to suck again. The height of this fixed amount overflow cylinder water level in all compartments associated plants therein (supplied plane).

Flooding plate structure

Table flood/flood plate and channel (rhythmic movement) determination of the nature of the system is invaluable when one must set the plants at the stage of the system, and they should move a ton of plants from the set in a more extensive operation. Flooded instead of separate compartments with plants therein, this technique satisfies only one of the headlines. Usually is placed on a table surface square compartment or square shape. The deposit, most of the time, is down directly with easy access.

Water is diverted to the top of the flooding of a deposit side plate, and the overflow is on the opposite side of the flume plate. This ensures that water is, of course, a side of the plate/panel to the other. As flood balanced with each flooding and the duct system (return), the height of the overflow tube defines the height of the water in the circulation, and may or less.

The plants were grown and placed in flood panels trimmed typical plants in pots or plastic containers standard. But the media in hydroponic development are circumcised, unlike natural plants for pot plants used instead of garden soil. When the plants are big enough, you can move in a perpetual hydroponic system.

A disadvantage of the table tide with the development of green growth and should be disposed of properly. It is left open from the highest point of the disc when the light is allowed in the supply of nutrients to the base of the plate to allow for the development of green growth. The only green growth is not right, however, usually used for plants, oxygen in the water broke.

Structure of the tank and a channel flow system (return) Serge

The type of arrangement of the mud flood expansion and the channel is beneficial when space is needed increasingly vertical. The systems commonly associated with flooding and the channel the deposit is still lower than in the hydroponic system. Therefore, water (nutrients available) again by the system to drain by gravity into the store by the overflow, and when the case is turned off. However, it may at least produce a flood channel system in all cases. When the water level in the reservoir is higher than the hydroponic system, it should be flooding and the removal of the vacuum. It is with the use of an expansion vessel.

The types of expenditure coolant reservoir flood channel and get more on the ground that there are many other necessary parts. The ability required by the head of the water seeks its level. The water level will be equivalent in a vehicle in another compartment when it is associated below the waterline. Clearing House as a buffer that controls the size of the water in all securities with plants filling in them and just packed during the flood cycle.

System serge tank flooding and the channel (repeating unit) is operated with a waterfall (nutrients available) from the central memory is much more abundant in the container when the siphon twill shows on. When the water level rises in the serge tank, the water level increases uniformly all plant holder is assigned simultaneously. When the water level is sufficiently high, a float valve in the reservoir a siphon twill turns in the serge tank. The siphon in the tank body this point of water siphons back into the necessary diet. Now both siphons (siphon in the first memory and the surge tank).

After the watch in the closed primary care, the siphon has not completed the siphon in the Serge tank yet. The siphon into the body tank retains all water siphon again in principle supply (system damaging) until the water level is sufficiently low. Then a second float valve twill around the siphon tank closes.

3. TECHNICAL nutrient film

Abstract technically within the meaning NFT (nutrient film technique) system.

The system can also be called NFT (nutrient film technique) is very famous with hydroponic growers at home. Mainly because of their original plan. However, NFT systems are used as the most appropriate and most used for the development of small plants rapidly developing different types of salad. With the development of lettuce, commercial manufacturers also different kinds of herbs and vegetables for children NFT systems developed.

Although there will be more opportunities to plan an NFT system, they all have a similar function of a nutrient agreeing on a decline exceptionally flat through the tube. When exposed, foundations plants underlie interact with water and can it retain nutrients. The major disadvantage of an NFT system is that the plants are susceptible to disturbances in the flow of river water outages (or whatever reason). Plants quickly begin to shrink when no more water flows through the system.

What you need to build an NFT system:

• Containers for the available nutrients (supply)

• underwater fountain/siphon lake

• dispersed water siphon hose to the development rollers NFT

• pipes for growth in plants thrive (also called a groove/channel)

Begin • solid starting shapes or small containers and Development Media seedlings

• a feedback system (pipes, channels) to control the arrangement of nutrients Auto Bazar

How simple system NFT is real. The provision of nutrients deviates upwards from the diet, most of the time, a complex that combines the most massive pipe a little different. Until the last of the small cylinder, the nutrient answer turns on one side of each of the channels/cracks in it with plants to develop. A sugar layer (film) of the provision of nutrient flow through each of the plants in the gaps on the opposite side, through each floor, and wetting the roots at the base of the channel, as is the case. The provision of nutrients from one side to the other based on the channel flow is slightly inclined so that the water flows down the inclination.

The growth of plant cylinders (channel/space) is usually beginning to adjusting the water on average start or small cubic inch small cavities in culture media at the highest point suspended cylinders. The base seedlings are hanging on the base of the cylinder/channel to flow down, where nutrients surface film obtained the supply of nutrients. The provision of nutrients overabundance low outflowing each channel to a circuit or downcomer and finishing to the tank where it is recirculated through the system.

Although the supply of nutrients to flow in the channel is flat, the mass of all roots root remains soaked plants can wick moisture away from the sources, also, as held by the humidity inside the cylinder/channel. Hearts that are between the bottom of the plant and the water level of moisture have been exposed in the channel reached, but to be on the other side, can be obtained by free oxygen-enriched air, also the lining of the cylinder/channel.

With extremely channels/grooves for CLS systems to the level of funds with gutters commercial along the way along with the channel breeders usually prepared. These notches allow water to flow to the root mass in the shelter and help to stagnate or reservoir. The manufacturer of vinyl rain downspouts household regularly drainage canals. These have comparable vinyl downspout sections. However, only a small amount of what I spend costs / did on the economic cycle neck. The manufacturer of round tubes also can widely use the ADS water system (Advanced Drainage System) for NFT Systems home. However, ADS tube has no grooves, with the extension of the

NFT flow system, and the inclination of the channel

What should the deep water, and how fast-flowing water to be the two most common questions that are asked of this type of system? First passes through the slope, how fast the water channel commands the cylinders/channel (not siphon or water).

The prescribed tendency to NFT is usually a 01-ratio: 30 to 1: 40. -TO we say (tilt) for all levels of the length of 30 to 40 scans, a thumbs case suggested. Beat their NFT systems planning; it is structured so that you can change the pitch, while the plants are still growing.

Indeed, as systems are more roots, they can bring to the pool and fire water to flow. If it is customizable, you can repair more if necessary, tilt. Also, in the assembly of CLS systems, try to keep the channel/trench is considered it wise would. The possibility that the items on the list, water goes in these regions.

Flow is proposed to NFT generally 1/4 gallon to half a gallon per time (1 to 2 l) is increased for each tube (channel / GAP). Or, secondly, from 15 gallons to 30 gallons per hour (60 to 120 liters). Although plants are seedlings can, the proposed rate is reduced by half, so extended that higher plants obtained.

Flux, as they have been much more upper or lower, sometimes brought malnutrition combined. Similarly, nutrient deficiency is sometimes observed when the growth is a cylinder (channel/throat) more than 30 to 40 feet (10 to 15 meters). Indeed

4. Water Culture

Hydroponic

Hydroponic systems are the most direct of all six types of hydroponic systems. Although unaffected, they remain an excellent success for hydroponic plants. Not only a ton of home producers makes hydroponic systems use. However, many commercial manufacturers use this type of system is also a big scale. Most of the time, because the hydroponic systems are a simple idea simple. It is also a kind of cheap manufacturing system and a different motivation behind it is too often with the producers of the house. Although the idea is simple,

You must mount a hydroponic system:

• Containers for the supply of nutrients (food)

• Aquarium suction device

• Airline/tube

• air stones (or soaker hose) to small airbags

Keeping • The baskets, glasses, and bowls plants

Some types of culture media •

As a hydroponic system works, it is merely water. The plant is available directly, suspended in the container on the nutrients in the memory. Most of the time, drive the styrofoam above or cut in the top of the cover storage holes. The roots hang bushel. The plants are directly related to the nutrients that they are immersed in. The origins always remain every minute of every day underwater. The roots are because they get stifling air and oxygen; they need air bubbles through the supply of nutrients and oxygen to the money in the rising water itself.

The air bubbles, for better water culture systems. Increase airbags should make the water bubbling water in an overwhelming bubble movement. Airbags were at the root and are obtained by growing as to the highest point of the water to rise better for plants. There are two different types of airflow and separation of oxygen on nutrient availability.

Types of airflow

Bubbles

A pneumatic machine and stones air aquarium are typically used airbags to provide an answer to hydroponic systems in nutrients, as well as various types of hydroponic systems. The vacuum device is the volume of air and is connected to vent with a carrier/tube. Air stones are made of a similar material permeable to the sand, and small pores are individual bubbles on the highest point of the water to rise (nutrients available).

A soaker hose can be used instead of air stones to air also increases. Irrigation hose air is significantly lower bubbles. Bubbles Littler, better circulation of air through the supply of nutrients.

Littler, the air bubbles are more in contact with the surface of the water. The connection between water and air pockets oxygen-free bumping money with plant roots added.

Waterfall

Even though the operation of the system in hydroponic systems for original equipment manufacturers, Surface disturbs the water spray case to another method, I generally suitable for air that circulates through the supply of nutrients. More water, and the volume of water that falls, the more power during descent, which makes the surface of the water. The downward force, the lower the air circulation, and the more disturbing it was (oxygen bankruptcy).

This strategy for the flow of air gradually conventional hydroponic systems business because they use large amounts of water as opposed to the producer of the house.

Recycling Culture Water Systems

Another variety of the execution of the watermill culture system is a water recycling culture system. The system operates as a recycling system of flooding and the channel; however, it is never exhausted. It may have the same number of compartments in the growth (harvest water deposits) to be connected to the need, with refractive power. Each compartment has its bottling increasingly as a channel of the tube channel/overflow, which concentrates the store.

Some manufacturers use boxes instead of liberal media and flat. Each with its factory in her thick and loaded with the available nutrients. You can have a line of this basin with a source-drain / siphon lake nutrient available for each cube. As the water fills the cans, the water overflows overflowing and flowing in the direction of the container, where it is recycled back through the system in the fullness of the cylinder.

Most growers recycle nutrients arrangement as for their cropping systems, only water in a central vacuum tank unit rather than on each box (mainly side box). Let water flows continuously siphon every minute of every day. However, if air bubbles are performed at each water tank universal culture system, the time may change in the waterfall. Also, the plants from direct contact benefit with the increase of air bubbles reach the roots.

Water allows the recycling, and the opportunity to test the water to use that falls as a source of airflow in the system. Likewise, you should not continue to the water level in each holder of repression check water plants drinking (just check and the central repository repressed), a reasonable advantage when you have large or many a plant grow similar system. Virtually all the major farming systems have water recycling industrial waterworks through the system.

DOC (more rooted water culture)

The term "DWC" is often misused when water is culture systems. So, what is a "DWC" and why not "DWC" six types of hydroponic systems? It is not only a kind of alternative hydroponic system through a stretch of the imagination. How was previously a hydroponic system is called by the name of "deep water culture," which is only a variety of existing type of hydroponic system obviously. can be used before "Deep," illustrate some hydroponic systems, when the depth of water in the order is lower than 8.10 inches. At this time, this property can an accurate DWC system are considered. Indeed

Often, its water / deep understanding of nutrients should not be deeper than 8 inches. This is important for large plants with more extensive root systems that require more space or perhaps drink a lot more water. Or, if a medium, such as a basin, to achieve high enough to fill the top of the root ball of the plant above the shutter used suitably. Plants such as the size of most salad box sets without much of a stretch of water just 4.6 traces grow hydroponic systems.

Today, finally, is the difference between how a culture system of ordinary water and DWC (deep water culture) work or the capabilities of the system. The same accuracy, the main difference between the two is the depth of water in the system. Regardless of whether an ordinary culture system water, an authentic DWC system, or even a standard recycled water culture or trustworthy DWC system, which, however, ensure that enough volume water and high oxygen to the root system to help plants. In any case, when they reach their full size.

The volume of water is unique tallness compared to water. If there occurs a gallon of water and poured into a large pool, the water level may be one or two inches in height, but that the casting of a gallon of water to a similar width of 3-inch cylinders, the height of water or more than two feet. Therefore, the water volume and elevation are two completely different things. It gradually on how much volume of water a plant, returning at this time to use "the required size. "

If the water level is above or below a bushel?

It is often confused and part of the time, perhaps jokes, where the level / available nutrients in the water must be water culture systems. The case should be with the water in contact or just hang on? There are advantages and disadvantages to both. However, there is no set-in-stone and tends to be. The water level is also is quick and secure in a hydroponic system to amend more water or take a little.

At the site where the bubbles reach the top of the water, flying over the surface of the water. Since the noise, spraying small water droplets of one or two inches above the surface of the water. As some of these tiny beads sprayed pool includes all depends, as actually expected much air, and therefore air bubbles that grow on the surface of the stones air.

If the container does not depend on contact with water and is just above these small grains sprayed water helps to keep the growth medium in the vicinity of the base of the last box. The amount of moisture is based on the number of airs bring is not broadcast and sprinkle the surface of the water near the surface. A check with bubbling water is correct cons (substantial heated movement is a bubble merely moving bubbly cooking). With significant progress, perfect balloons, and easy dampened negligibly. Another issue is the type of media being used increasingly. Some culture media to absorb moisture and decision-making faster and more efficiently than others,

something when hungover, and this can sometimes be an advantage at the point where the tank in contact with water, the culture media can be added to the boxing / more water. Anyway, again, it has the kind of growing media a significant impact, because some culture media ingest moisture storage and faster and easier than others. In this way, it can entirely with water tank near the bottom of the case are saturated with inconsistent contact with water. If so, cut just to the water level so that the cans above the water instead are suspended, or use an alternative culture media type.

It is also essential to refer to the size of the plant also affects. The roots of the plant grow elimination forfeited water/nutrients. This means that they go and wherever moisture to grow. The possibility that the system is small, and not handed over the roots from the bottom of the box, however, it may be advantageous to have contact tank with water. In any case, up until the origins of the base and long enough to stay underwater.

In all cases, if the base of the cubes is excellent and of many small droplets of water into the air around the bubble burst sprayed cooked while suspended above the water. Additional moisture ball essential nutrient media root plants unceremoniously assembly /, while the container in contact with water is absorbing water nutrients, growth can accelerate the roots. In contrast, the plant and root mass are still small.

Method Kratky

Anyway, first, I need to explain the call Kratky strategy is anything but a different type of hydroponic system. Notes that the argument that it is "supposedly" the only variety of standard hydroponic systems. But he sometimes refers generally a person's name (the name change. Supposedly the range should be named after the procedure Kratky BA at the University of Hawaii, who does not teach strategies hydroponic recycling.

No hydroponic recycling systems (more like referring "rush to squander" methods) course store unavailable water/nutrients for plants and the tank. They disregard any water from the siphon from the tank to the plant but then allow / nutrient response to the water channel on the floor or in a system of canals for spills. This seems inefficient. However, methods Recycling not be instrumental and has, if done correctly, virtually no side effects. Water management systems, by definition, are not recycling. You can, however, also be modified to flow systems.

A hydroponic system, called in some cases Kratky strategy is essentially a hydroponic system without the air pump in the NFT system. It is a hydroponic system because the plants store hanging fly water/nutrient roots down. It is also the NFT system part, because, as the CLS systems, a hole between the shell is the plant and water keep sitting the roots. This hole is to replace an air cushion and the vacuum device to a water level in the culture system.

Although plants are few bushels should touch the water, so that the roots grow from the base began. Since this type of plant roots grow and more, the plant takes on some of the water. This lowers to leave an air pocket the water level. Without the vacuum apparatus oxygen decomposed and to replace oxygen, the water, the plants need to get the air hole, the ability to transport oxygen. This type of system configuration is useful in places where power is unavailable or moody.

However, these techniques have their drawbacks unique. The machine reached separate air hydroponic systems, and the oxygen supply is interrupted. Rising airbags also keep the water moving. By the time available to the water/nutrients is faulty, mineral salts (nutrients) located near the base, after that gender imbalanced nutrient (potent at the bottom, and extremely low at the top). The air rises to the top of the development replenisher mixture vacuum device kept constant availability of nutrients and nutrients in the water to spread evenly.

Similarly, while the plants are bound, oxygen can be obtained if the technique Kratky is used to the roots of the waterline cannot get the nutrients. The sources below the waterline, not oxygen, are received, and that they are simply the oxygen in the water is exhausted early stages solved, and there is nothing to replace. This is a concern for the plant. We believe it is like to be in the pool and not have the ability to move, while his nose out of the water so he could breathe, and the mouth does not dry under the water line and ready to drink water, so. It can support along these lines in the way that you need, but

The plants are versatile and continuously try to adapt their condition and environment, as well as expected. However, given the circumstances when the Kratky strategy is not using proper condition by far. As it passes now from perfect health and a pneumatic machine every day or possibly to run in all cases, replace oxygen up bankrupt is extremely low. In areas where power is wholly irregular or non-existent, the Kratky technology may be an advantageous and useful option.

5. aeroponics system

Although the idea of the aeroponic system is straightforward, which specializes in all six types of hydroponic systems, the most are. However, it is still straightforward to build your essential aeroponic system, and a ton of home farmers to grow like, and to get good results, this type of hydroponic system.

A similar system with other hydroponic, a wide range may type of materials for their production, and a large number are used by types of network structure to fit into space. His have extremely limited by the area you and your creative spirit.

Some attractions in the vicinity of an aeroponic system are regularly used by the media, almost no growth. The roots receive more oxygen, and the plants grow faster that way. Similarly, aeroponic systems typically use less water than any other hydroponic system (particularly evident aeroponic systems). Likewise, the harvest is usually more natural, especially for roots.

There are some setbacks to aeroponic systems. It is also more expensive to produce. The heads of the RIE / sprinkler can stop mineral components in the supply of nutrients work broken. So, try to have attracted additional elements close when obstructed during cleaning.

Also, the fact is that the plants established hung by the structure of aeroponic systems in the air, the plant roots are much more vulnerable desiccation when an interruption of the irrigation cycle. Therefore, a brief power outage can even (in any case), the plant bite dust could be much faster than any other hydroponic system.

Furthermore

What you need to do your basic aeroponic system:

• Containers for the available nutrients (deposit).

• Siphon source/lake diving.

• The water pipe siphon Spread the heads of the Lord dine in the growth chamber.

• Closed growth chamber for the root zone.

• Mr. heads/sprinklers.

• A sealed chamber into the water and the expansion chamber, where it is the root system of the plant.

• The pipelines on excess nutrients available to restore the memory.

• The timer (ideally a clock cycle) to kill and siphon.

Like the aeroponic system is a straightforward idea. First, the motivation is behind the float in the air roots, it that the extreme measure of oxygen can get. The high volume of oxygen to the roots enables the design to grow faster than they otherwise would and do the main advantage of this type of hydroponic system.

Second, there is almost no regularity when a culture medium used, all naked to leave the roots of the plant. The plants are suspended in small capsules bushel or closed-cell foam or wrapped around the trunk of the plant. These little boxes or connections foam shaped openings on the highest growth chamber developed. Roots and injected into the expansion chamber with several nutrients' heads of the men in the standard short cycles. Regular watering cycles keep moist and the sources to give drying the same nutrients that plants need to grow.

It should be the roots of the culture chamber easily and be highlighted almost impenetrable. Allow outside air must, so that the roots get plenty of oxygen, but shed no need to water or to go pests. Similarly, the source of the camera is to be expected needed moisture. Finally, what you need is the root of a lot of moisture, fresh, to get oxygen and nutrients. A round of their scheduled aeroponic system is a decent parity of all three of these components to the roots simultaneously.

Finally, a central point in the aeroponic system is the size of water beads. Roots rain a mist fine much faster, thicker, and assimilates nutrients mounting surface and oxygen to the sources with small waves of water that the little heads of the sprinkler sprinkled to grow. What is the refuge of culture, even faster plants? Size beads of water sort types of aeroponic systems.

CHAPTER 13:

There Are Three Types Of Aeroponic Systems.

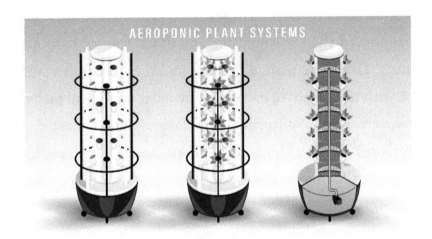

Underweight aeroponic systems (soakaponics)

Are in the same mode "soakaponics" aeroponic systems known under the weight of what many people see when an aeroponic exam. -With, i.e., primarily because most aeroponic systems in shops underweight supplies sold systems. While the systems work comfortably under the weight of the enormous size of the pearl, water is very different from the weight systems.

The primary explanation aeroponic underweight systems are so popular is that they do not need much in the way of costs or rare equipment, the different types of hydroponic systems. The simplicity and ease of lightweight systems are such attractive aeroponic systems for many producers of the house.

Even if you do not have to worry about any unusual or exceptional art water siphon, Source Standard / Lake will be beautiful and functional. However, you need a siphon, which is more rooted than it would for any other type of hydroponic system. This is the main difference and the most important. In fact, with the weight of each drip sprinkler system all included. However, give Wellspring and lake siphon unrated PSI (pressure), the GPH (gallons per hour) can be set closer to the "level of the maximum head," the ground (more weight) Siphon.

They are enough sprinkler heads must inject shields, and covers the entire root zone even if the plants get root mass bigger and bigger. Since the root mass is large, it is challenging to adjust sprinkler heads spray water to infiltrate the mass of thick roots. When the low weight of the structure of the aeroponic system so that the roots or rain near its highest point on the root mass, is the water through the root ball flows far superior to try the spray from below.

High weight aeroponic systems (real aeroponic systems)

While systems aeroponic systems underweight are best known to the high weight are systems "real" aeroponics. This is

B it atomizes the highest importance (60-90 psi) takes correctly with a small bead size water in a fine mist. This fine mist leaves the roots far more oxygen will get underweight systems as well. But gradually and involved expensive to mount the aeroponic system weight.

What you need to do your own aeroponic high real weight system:

• storage tank (further when the pressure of the storage tank).

• The solenoid valve (on top of the line opening and closing the supply level).

• Duty (for opening and closing the pipe).

• Spray M. (the roots with excellent mist irrigation).

• Small air blower (to the collection tank under pressure).

• Closed growth chamber for the root zone.

• An oil spill on the possibility of offering cover that they will recycle the nutrients.

Although the basic structure of the camera and plant cultivation support can still with the same underweight systems on. The water supply system is (nutrients available) completely different. Because of the frequency with which they need a siphon (100 to 1000 times per day) to kill, a product would be fast. Thus, the water trap is removed in the aeroponic system higher weight.

These fed printing. The easiest way to do this is a kind of collection reservoir in the RO water systems (flip-up) used to use. It is essentially only a container with the interior of the stomach elastic / separator so that different sides. Water (nutrients arrangements) is compressed on the one hand and the air in the other. The atmosphere is filled until the weight is about 60 psi to 90th. This weight pushes against an elastic stomach and is under pressure, the supply side with the nutrients in a similar psi.

A water line from the supply header of the expert in the encapsulation chamber extending the root growth of fogging. A solenoid valve is opened and uses the flow of water through the headers M line close. Planning opening and closing of the solenoid valve is controlled by a clock cycle. The clock cycle, the magnetic coil as little as one second, how open the crop demand and close. It is normal/open for a few moments, another after, when for a few minutes before splashing back. The clock cycle opens and closes the roots of garden plants magnets with fog in this kind of "on/off cycle" throughout the day.

Ultrasonic

Ultrasonic, was also be used for fog in aeroponic systems, but with mixed results. An ultrasonic nebulizer is most used for visual shows in lakes, etc. are used to an audience. They also sold around Halloween with Halloween decorations regularly. While making a mist with small beads of water, there is almost no actual moisture in the fog/mist.

The mist ultrasonic usually fall well to the support base. Therefore, it is difficult to ensure that the constant fog fully insures the roots. Another problem with the use of nebulizers that the leaves usually stop with the mineral form. The main panels that work have proved with impeccable quality are the heads of the most expensive Teflon. It can here to clean and use white vinegar or water and the pH down and to clean with a Q-tip. Some manufacturers have the ultrasonic helps consolidate aeroponic weight structure under a similar system.

6. BIT SYSTEM

Wick system

The wick system is less difficult for each of the six types of hydroponic systems. This is because they have no moving parts usually not used in this direction, the traps or performance. However, some people are still using the custom vacuum device in the repository.

Not worry about having the workforce is also very useful in places where the performance or capricious cannot be used.

The wick system is to learn a simple way the first production system hydroponics, and just diving to consider his need first. This type of hydroponic system is used by educators as a home room-tests for children regularly. So, to clarify for help to the growth of plants, and others who inspire them hydroponically.

You must mount a wick system:

• a tin or support for the plant.

• A tin or carrier deposition.

• Large takes the culture media such as coconut Coco, vermiculite, perlite, or.

Some parts of the absorbent material such as rope or large felt •.

How does it look like the wick system; it seems, which is mostly absorbed by the supply of nutrients to plants using the method of hair activity. Which means that absorbs water to plants through the wick as a wipe. In general, large wick systems, in each case, at least two strands of enough size to supply the water plant (nutrient response). The hub/support with the ground is substantially directly above the compartment for food. The water should go this way, not far a feasible means of communication to find with plants.

The drawback schemes mecha

The main disadvantage of a wick system usually does not work great for large plants that need more water to drink. Setting growing very progressively smaller plants, not fertile like lettuce and herbs. While absorbed lock (lock-up) moisture to the plant roots, the more the plant to drink, the more water. Random what they are fruit plants, they need the growth of any retention of water and fruit a lot more water to help.

Wick systems also have the disadvantage that they effectively less to transport nutrients. More massive plants need nutrients to promote faster than Wicks roots can provide. Lettuce and herbs to eat usually mild, are very greedy for plants like tomatoes, peppers, and most fruit plants.

Another disadvantage of the lock system is that the plants cannot ingest nutrients and water pretty, and the wick not determine what the plant needs nutrients. Plants absorb the nutrients and water they need and leave the rest of the nutrients in the culture medium. This can lead to a deadly development of mineral salts in the culture media at the end. Therefore, crisp washing of nutrients from the abundance of the root zone (press) regularly with water, such as once a week or something like that.

Highlights

The castle itself is probably the essential part of the wick system, arguing that do not get a decent bit spongy, plants, the moisture, and nutrients it needs. You probably do some testing of different materials to see what works best for you. When looking for suitable absorbent material, something should use that remains, however, it is still waterproof prey. To wash this time the large wick before use, you can improve the ability to spread from most materials.

Some people base materials that have wick systems have been things used as fibrous cord. Propylene felt strips, and tiki burned Wicks, rayon cord or mop head strands interlaced polyurethane yarn, wool felt, rope or pieces of wool, nylon rope, cotton rope, the texture of the old tape dress or ceiling and so on and so on.

Make the use of plants to unload enough help for water a point. This depends on how the wick system, the type of plant breeding, and the means are increasingly produced. You probably in all cases except if it is a genuine 02/04 evacuation binary system. Similarly, the shorter wick water to the store must go to the media and roots develop, the more water that you send to the culture media.

When the arrangement of nutrients makes the wick of the culture medium, it is necessary to use a culture medium permeable to help absorb moisture and retention. The mean of the absolute culture is generally used for wick systems are things like Coco coir, vermiculite, perlite, or. Sometimes, water-absorbing polymer, even precious stones are also used.

The Reservoir

The storage system wick can be large or small, and simply do not have to run dry. Should Moreover, it is necessary to keep the relatively high-water level, so that water (nutrients available) does not rise much a rhythm, and rhizosphere media are possible. You must stop the supply of nutrients with the new array variable and completely wipe and sometimes turn. It argues that green growth and microorganisms can begin to grow in nutrient-rich water, especially if it is not a confirmation of light.

Since the wick absorbed relatively water and nutrients, and use the plants or do not consume consistently, a development glut nutrient can grow in culture media after a while. So, you may have to wash with clean water also generally fragile. Chances are something like about every two weeks. The probability of development will reduce from nutritious and reach harmful levels of salts for plants.

Discretion suction device

The use of a vacuum device and the vent airflow through the water in a wick system is unimportant. However, it can be useful. While the roots should oxygen small pockets of air in the culture medium, but they retain oxygen up to self-bankruptcy water itself as well as can get. In addition to the airflow through the water, moving to help, and increased airflow pockets of still water. Retention of nutrients in the water moves maintains approximately uniformly stirred continuously for nutrients. If the water continues to be, based nutrients can regulate after a specific time. However, it uses a vacuum device in the case,

Conclusion Part 1

If you have read this far this, I can see that you start serious about your own hydroponic garden at home. Well done! You have taken the first step and the most important, get all the information you need. Now you can go ahead and start making a list of plants to grow. Then make a small list of some basic items you need to buy the home or to install and you are ready.

I also want to congratulate the right decision. The advantages of hydroponics are often used. It will help now to a healthy environment. In the first example is the use of pesticides, the component of most traditional agricultural methods is eliminated.

Due to the growth of plants in a controlled room, you should not have any problem with the noise. Vegetables are fully organically grown, it that you and your family first put.

Secondly, far fewer resources are required to develop their vegetables if your hydroponic methods.

The water is used for the nutrient solution recycled and reused, which means using less. No compromises occur spill that the environment and traditional gardening can harm.

Finally, Hydroponic gardening is a lot less work. He is working on a compact space and can organize all your plants at waist level, so you have on your knees do not go or rejects all the time. You will also save a lot of time.

With all these benefits in mind, I am sure it is to convince no need. So, go out and start over. Before long, you will be able to get their first harvest to harvest and enjoy your wonderful healthy harvest vegetables, full of flavor and goodness. Not only will you impress your friends with their organic products, but you can only convince their own hydroponic gardens as well as to begin, especially when they see how it easy and space-saving without chaos.

Hydroponics is difficult to cultivate a method. In fact, it is so effective, you will quickly see why people want to make the extra effort that their plants grow in this way. Is do not be intimidated by any science; in fact, if you stand on your head, hydroponic store like to give you a basic layout and clarify anything that does not receive.

If you start to get some first operating system in this way, once you get the hang, less likely to kill the monitoring a love harvest.

We hope that you have learned a lot about the main components of hydroponics and as always to obtain the best plants. The next step is the system runs to get lucky!

CPSIA information can be obtained
at www.ICGtesting.com
Printed in the USA
BVHW081205091220
595274BV00012B/1520